Wind and Water

by Jim Ollhoff

Visit us at
WWW.ABDOPUBLISHING.COM

Published by ABDO Publishing Company, 8000 West 78th Street, Suite 310, Edina, MN 55439. Copyright ©2010 by Abdo Consulting Group, Inc. International copyrights reserved in all countries. No part of this book may be reproduced in any form without written permission from the publisher. ABDO & Daughters™ is a trademark and logo of ABDO Publishing Company.

Printed in the United States of America, North Mankato, Minnesota
102009
012010

 PRINTED ON RECYCLED PAPER

Editor: John Hamilton
Graphic Design: John Hamilton
Cover Photos: Jupiter Images, iStockphoto
Interior Photo: Getty Images, p. 6, 7, 11, 17; John Hamilton, p. 9; iStockphoto, p. 1, 4, 5, 8, 10, 12, 13, 14, 15, 18, 20, 22, 23, 24, 25, 26, 27, 29; TVA, p. 16; U.S. Army Corps of Engineers, p. 21.

Library of Congress Cataloging-in-Publication Data

Ollhoff, Jim, 1959-
  Wind and water / Jim Ollhoff.
    p. cm. -- (Future energy)
  Includes index.
  ISBN 978-1-60453-939-4
  1. Wind power--Juvenile literature. 2. Water-power--Juvenile literature. I. Title.
  TJ820.O484 2010
  621.4'5--dc22
                    2009029859

Contents

Wind and Water

Wind and water are two of the most plentiful things on the earth. Could our energy needs be met, in part, by these two powerful resources?

As the world's industries and homes demand more and more electricity, power plants burn more coal and other fossil fuels. Burning fossil fuels pollutes the earth and puts carbon into the air. Most scientists believe that more carbon in our atmosphere leads to higher climate temperatures, which could put the world in crisis.

Below: Wind power is one of the cleanest energy sources available.

But clean, renewable energy sources are available. Renewable sources create very little pollution, and they don't ever run out. Wind and water could produce a large part of our energy needs today.

Windmills currently produce less than one percent of the electricity needs in North America. However, wind power is growing rapidly. In fact, wind power is the cleanest energy source on the planet, and the fastest-growing renewable source.

Hydroelectric power creates electricity when flowing water spins turbines. This generates electricity cleanly and without pollutants. Hydroelectric power has been around for a long time, and its use can grow.

Together, wind and water could help us create a cleaner future. Wind and water probably will not be able to meet 100 percent of our energy needs in the near future. However, they will be an important part of the solution to a world in crisis.

Below: Hydroelectric power is a proven technology that produces electricity relatively cleanly.

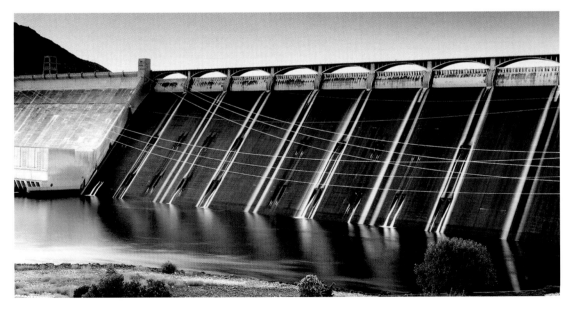

History of Wind Power

People have been using the power of the wind since history began. Sailors used the wind to move their boats before motors were invented.

The windmill gets its name from early machines invented in Persia and China, possibly 500 AD or earlier. Farmers needed to grind grain into flour, which is called "milling" the grain. They used the wind as a way to power the grinding machines. In the Netherlands, the Dutch became famous for building windmills that not only milled grains, but also pumped water out of the ground.

Below: A row of windmills next to a canal in the Netherlands.

In the 1870s, many farmers in the United States were using windmills to pump water. This was used for home water and for farm animals. In the 1880s, windmills began to be used to generate electricity. The use of electric generation grew for several decades. However, by the 1930s, most communities were connected to the power grid. The grid—still in use today—generates electricity mostly from cheap and reliable fossil fuels such as coal. Electricity from windmills slowly faded away.

In the 1970s, there was a brief "energy crisis." Foreign countries stopped delivering oil to the United States. Immediately, the government began to invest in wind power. However, when the oil crisis eased, government funds for wind power were scaled back. Industries returned to fossil fuels to generate electricity.

Today, the problems with fossil fuels have created a new kind of crisis. Wind power is once again becoming important as we look to the future.

Below: An abandoned farm near Colorado Springs, Colorado.

Modern Windmills

Modern windmills have three parts: the tower, the blades, and a box called a nacelle, which contains equipment that converts the wind motion into electricity.

The towers are tall structures that form the base of the windmill and hold the blades. Since wind blows faster at higher altitudes, the higher the tower, the better. Older windmill towers have a lattice style, which looks like a ladder. Modern windmills have tubular towers, which make them safer for birds and bats.

The blades of the windmills are usually made from fiberglass. In newer windmills, carbon or glass is sometimes added. This makes the blades stronger and lighter.

Traditional windmills have blades that are oriented up and down. The axis on which those blades spin turns horizontally, or parallel to the ground, so it is called a horizontal windmill. Some newer windmills have a vertical design, so the axis on which the blades spin is vertical to the ground. Some newer small windmills don't have blades at all, but just a tall sleeve that spins vertically.

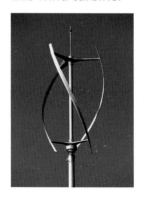

Below: A vertical axis wind turbine.

AT THE TOP OF THE TOWER IS THE NACELLE. IT CONTAINS EQUIPMENT THAT CONVERTS MOTION INTO ELECTRICITY.

TYPICAL BLADE LENGTH IS ABOUT 80 FEET (24 M)

FIBERGLASS-REINFORCED POLYESTER BLADE

TYPICAL HEIGHT OF TOWER IS ABOUT 200 FEET (61 M)

TUBULAR STEEL TOWER

THE WIND FARM AT CERRO GORDO, IOWA, PRODUCES ENOUGH ELECTRICITY TO POWER MORE THAN 20,000 HOMES AND BUSINESSES ANNUALLY.

On top of the tower, next to the windmill blades, is a box-like structure called a nacelle. Inside is the power converter. Its job is to change the motion of the blades into electricity. It is an advanced piece of electronic equipment. It has to adjust to different wind speeds, make electricity, and feed the electricity into wires so that it can be distributed to the utility companies.

The electricity has to be at the right voltage so the power lines and the electric grid can handle it. But the wind blows at different speeds, generating different voltages. Some windmills fix this problem by forcing the blades to spin at the same rate, no matter how fast the wind blows. Some newer windmills electronically change the voltage to meet the needs of the grid. Most windmills shut down automatically if the wind blows too fast.

Below: A cutaway diagram of the interior of a wind turbine, revealing the intricate series of gears and electronic equipment needed to produce electricity.

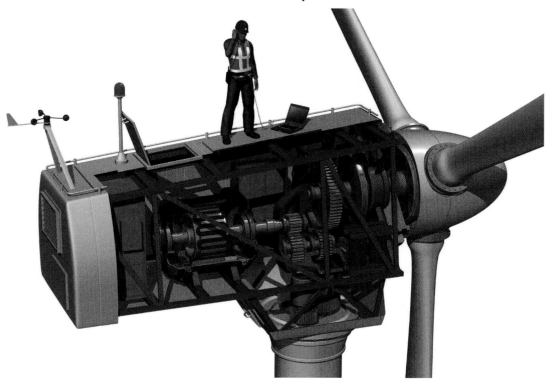

In some states, the power grid is very old, and can't handle the on-again, off-again nature of the wind. In many places, the power grid needs to be updated.

The ocean is a great place for wind power. Some companies are building windmills offshore because it is almost always windy there.

Sometimes, the windiest places are farthest from where the electricity is needed. States like Montana, Wyoming, and North Dakota are very windy, but have smaller populations and don't need very much electricity. Transmission lines have to be built to move the electricity to the places that need it.

Several countries in Europe are ahead of North America in using wind power. Countries such as Denmark, Spain, and Germany have a large amount of their energy needs met with wind power.

Above: Turbines of an offshore wind farm at dusk, off the coast of Wales, United Kingdom. The ocean is often a good place for turbines because of reliably windy conditions.

Advantages of Wind Power

The biggest advantage of wind power is that it is a renewable source of power. It won't ever run out, unlike oil or natural gas.

Wind power is the cleanest source of power in the world. Other renewables create small environmental problems. Hydroelectric power can displace the natural habitats of many animals. Solar power creates a small amount of pollution in the making of solar panels, although the pollution created is much, much less than burning fossil fuels. There is no perfectly clean energy source, but wind power is the cleanest and has the least impact on the environment.

Left: A cluster of wind turbines with their blades in motion.

Another advantage is that small windmill units can be placed on individual houses and businesses. This allows houses or businesses to use energy directly from windmills, and then buy the rest of their electricity from the public power utility. A small windmill might provide a quarter of the energy needs of an average house. If the house was very energy efficient, it's possible that a small windmill might provide all the electricity the home needs.

In northwest Missouri, there is a small town called Rock Port, with about 1,300 residents. A few people decided to do something about clean energy. So, in 2006 they built four large windmills to power their town. It turned out that the windmills produced more electricity than the town needed. It became the first city in North America to get all its electricity from wind power.

Above: A domestic wind generator supplements the electrical power of a private home in the United Kingdom.

Wind Power Problems

One disadvantage of wind power is that the towers are big and bulky. While everyone likes the idea of wind power, many people say, "Not in my backyard." Sometimes windmills are noisy, especially older models. Many people don't like the towers near their property.

Below: Birds can be killed by flying into the spinning blades of wind turbines, but pet cats kill many times more birds than do windmills.

Bird kills are often cited as a problem, although they are not as bad a problem as most people think. A few thousand birds are killed each year when they crash into windmill blades. To put this in perspective, more than 100 million birds are killed each year by cats in the United States. Approximately 50 to 100 million birds die by crashing into cars and trucks.

While bird kills are a problem, bat kills are a bigger problem. Biologists have yet to do a complete study on the issue, but it seems that more bats, rather than birds, are killed by windmills. Bats don't crash into the blades of windmills. Instead, because bats have very sensitive lungs, when they fly near a moving windmill blade, their lungs are damaged by the air pressure changes, fatally injuring them. A decline in bats would be a problem because each bat eats thousands of insect pests, which damage crops. Scientists hope that newer vertical windmills will be less of a problem for bats.

Above: A sky full of bats emerging from a cave near San Antonio, Texas. Bats eat insect pests that damage crops. If too many bats are killed by windmills, crop yields might suffer.

Electricity From Water

The ancient Greeks used flowing water to turn small turbines, which would grind grain. Since then, the power of flowing water has been used for many things, such as moving cranes, running textile equipment, and blasting away hillsides. Today, hydropower, or hydroelectric power, is used to move turbines that generate electricity. More than 20 percent of the world's energy comes from hydropower.

Large hydropower plants can be found on many rivers. Usually, engineers build dams on rivers with a steep drop in elevation. The dam creates a large lake, called a reservoir. Water from the reservoir then falls through a large tube called a penstock, where it turns the propeller-like blades of a huge turbine. The rotating turbine forces the metal shaft of an electric generator to spin. The generator creates electricity, which is then transported by power lines.

Facing page: Arizona's Glen Canyon Dam, on the Colorado River. *Below:* A cutaway diagram of a large hydroelectric plant.

RESERVOIR

INTAKE

PENSTOCK

GENERATOR

TURBINE

POWER LINES

RIVER

Above: A row of electric generators inside Hoover Dam.

A good example of a large hydropower plant is Hoover Dam, which is on the Colorado River near Las Vegas, Nevada. Engineers started building the dam in 1933. The massive concrete structure is 726 feet (221 m) tall. The building of the dam created a reservoir of water called Lake Mead. The reservoir is 110 miles (177 km) long, and is a popular recreation destination. Electricity from Hoover Dam is sent to Arizona and California, as well as Nevada.

Most of the large rivers in the United States are already being used to generate hydroelectric power. However, there are many places where smaller hydropower plants can still be created.

Another kind of hydropower is sometimes called hydrokinetic energy. This takes advantage of natural movements of water, such as ocean tides, currents, and waves. Hydrokinetic power does not yet provide much electricity, but it has vast possibilities for energy in the future. Wave power facilities in Sweden, Portugal, and the United States have been very successful. Scientists are experimenting with different technologies for hydrokinetic power. One design resembles an underwater windmill that spins as tides move water back and forth.

Hydrokinetic energy could eventually generate power for areas along the Pacific and Atlantic Coasts. It is a rapidly growing technology that could someday account for large amounts of electricity.

Below: The front end of a Pelamis Wave Energy Converter bursts through a wave off the shores of Portugal.

Small Hydropower Sytems

Another type of hydropower is called small hydropower, or micro-hydropower systems. These are very small electric generators. In some cases, they can power a small community. Sometimes, they are so small they only power a single house, or just part of a house.

The design of these small hydropower systems can be as simple as a wheel that rotates when water flows

Below: A stream powering a waterwheel, which runs an electric generator inside a log cabin.

past it. These waterwheels are strong enough to power turbines and generators, which create electricity. These hydropower systems are called damless hydroelectric designs.

Another design, sometimes called run-of-the-river hydroelectricity, uses the natural current of the river, instead of falling water from a dam. Water from the river's current is fed through pipes, which turns turbines. Sometimes, run-of-the-river designs have small dams, but without a large reservoir. A big advantage of the smaller damless hydropower plants is that they don't disrupt natural habitats the way large dams do.

A good thing about small hydropower systems is that homes that use them don't use as much energy from public utilities. Since early in the twentieth century, the approach to energy has been to get all electricity from a central power plant grid. Small hydropower, windmills, and solar energy collectors are ways to get electricity other than from a central grid.

Above: The Chief Joseph Dam near Bridgeport, Washington, is an example of a run-of-the-river power station. There is no sizable reservoir behind the dam.

Advantages of Energy From Water

I n a large hydropower system, electricity can be created at a constant rate. When electricity isn't needed, engineers can close pipes that carry water to the turbines. If more electricity is needed, more pipes can be opened.

The reservoir behind the dam can be used for many purposes. It can be used for irrigation in farm fields. Some reservoirs, such as Lake Mead at Hoover Dam, are popular destinations for fishing, boating, skiing, and recreation. Dams can also buffer seasonal water changes, helping control spring flooding, for example.

Left: A waterskier on Lake Powell, a reservoir straddling the border between Arizona and Utah. Lake Powell was created by the construction of the Glen Canyon Dam on the Colorado River.

Water is a renewable resource. Fossil fuels, such as oil, will eventually run out. Water is also available in North America. We don't need to buy it from foreign countries. Hydropower is also cheaper than fossil fuels—about half the cost.

Another advantage is the potential of the newer types of hydropower. Technology for getting power from waves or tides is rapidly growing, and shows great promise for the future.

Perhaps most importantly, the actual generation of electricity from water does not produce pollutants or greenhouse gasses. No toxic chemicals are put into the air or water.

Above: Hoover Dam, with Lake Mead behind it.

Hydropower Problems

While the actual generation of electricity from water does not produce any greenhouse gasses, the reservoirs of large dams can produce these gasses. Decaying plants and other organic material deep beneath the water produce carbon dioxide and methane. Both of these are powerful greenhouse gasses. The amount is small compared to fossil fuel-burning plants, but it still contributes to the greenhouse effect and climate change.

Large hydroelectric dams need large reservoirs. These large bodies of water often displace plants and animals from their natural habitat. Some fish, such as salmon, need to swim upstream to spawn, and large dams can get in their way. Biologists sometime build a long series of steps, called fish ladders, so that fish can get around dams, but they don't always work.

Below: A fish ladder constructed next to Bonneville Dam on the Columbia River, between Washington and Oregon.

Run-of-the-river hydroelectric facilities don't use large dams. But when there is a drought, the rivers may dry up. When there is no water, there is no electricity.

The unintended consequences of wave and tidal power are still unknown. Will the underwater machinery harm marine life? Or will it have some other effect on fishing or marine life?

Below: Lake Mead, just above Hoover Dam. The white rocks show how much the water level has dropped in recent years.

Transistion to Wind and Water

Below: A high-voltage power station.

One thing that would make the switch to wind and water happen more quickly is government policy. The government could provide tax credits and other supportive policies for the renewable power industry.

This would cut down on the high upfront costs of manufacturing new windmills or hydropower plants.

Another thing that would help is updating the power transmission infrastructure. This means that the power lines, electrical towers, and transformers that link the utility companies to homes and businesses need to be updated. Some parts of today's electrical grid are very old. Some parts of the grid, for example, have a difficult time with wind energy, which varies with how the wind blows.

Above: A home with its own wind power generator.

Engineers and scientists will also need to work closely with biologists to understand how to minimize harmful effects on animal life. How can they build a windmill that is safe for birds and bats? How can they build a hydroelectric plant that is safe for fish? These are important issues that need to be addressed as engineers seek to provide electricity but also protect the environment.

Finally, decentralizing our electric generation would help the switch to wind and water. Right now, most of the electric grid is centralized. This means that one power plant produces electricity for an entire community. To decentralize means to have many places that generate electricity. If every house had a small windmill, for example, that would be a decentralized grid. There would still be a central electric plant to generate power when the wind isn't blowing, but the size of the central plant could be much smaller.

The Future of Wind and Water Power

Humans always have an impact on the environment. Everything we do has consequences. The big question is, "How can we make the least harmful impact?" Energy from wind and water has consequences, but the impact is far less than obtaining energy from burning fossil fuels.

Could engineers create floating windmills on the ocean that deliver power with a cable? Could scientists create an offshore bank of windmills and wave generators? Could communities put small, vertical windmills on every home and business? Could engineers work with biologists to put small hydrokinetic turbines in every river? Could scientists put windmills in windy, isolated areas and use highly efficient power lines to get the electricity where it is needed?

There are many ways to collect electricity with wind and water. The technology is mostly there. The resources—wind and water—are available. Leadership is needed to create a new world of electricity. The future of electricity from wind and water is bright.

Facing page: A large wind turbine farm at sunset. The immediate future of renewable forms of energy, both wind and water, seems bright.

Glossary

CARBON DIOXIDE

Normally a gas, carbon dioxide is a chemical compound made up of two oxygen atoms and one carbon atom. Its chemical symbol is CO_2. Carbon dioxide in the earth's atmosphere acts as a greenhouse gas.

DAMLESS HYDROPOWER

Small hydropower plants that don't create dams and large reservoirs on rivers, but allow the normal flow of the river to turn a turbine, which generates electricity. It is sometimes called run-of-the-river hydropower.

ELECTRIC GRID

Power lines, transformers, transmission substations, and all of the parts of the system that bring electricity from a power plant into people's homes.

FOSSIL FUEL

Fuels that are created by the remains of ancient plants and animals that were buried and then subjected to millions of years of heat, pressure, and bacteria. Oil and coal are the most common fossil fuels burned to create electricity. Natural gas is also a fossil fuel. Burning fossil fuels releases carbon dioxide into the atmosphere, contributing to global warming.

GENERATOR

A machine that turns mechanical energy, such as blowing wind or falling water, into electricity.

GREENHOUSE EFFECT

The earth naturally warms because of the greenhouse effect. The surface of the earth absorbs some solar radiation, and reflects some. The reflected rays either pass back into space, or are absorbed and reflected back by gasses in the earth's atmosphere. Carbon dioxide is a major greenhouse gas that is produced by burning fossil fuels. When too much solar radiation is absorbed, the earth warms up, which alters climates around the world.

GREENHOUSE GAS

Any gas that is good at absorbing and retaining the sun's heat. Carbon dioxide, which is released into the atmosphere by the burning of fossil fuels, is a greenhouse gas.

HYDROPOWER

Any method that creates electricity from the flowing of water.

NACELLE

The part of the windmill at the top of the tower that contains the equipment that converts the motion of the blades into electricity.

RENEWABLE ENERGY

Any kind of energy where the source won't get used up. Wind power, waterpower, and solar power are examples of renewable energy.

VERTICAL WINDMILL

A relatively new kind of windmill, in which the axis that turns the blades spins vertical to the ground. Traditional windmills have a blade axis that is parallel to the ground, with the blades swinging up and down in a circle.

Index